6

D0786421

PUPPET and Pantomime PLAYS

The ultimate in puppetry is reached when you can create puppets like Magnolia Ostrich and Calvin Crow, who appear on the *Family Show,* an NBC television feature. The puppeteers are Paul and Mary Ritts.

PUPPET and
Pantomime
PLAYS

By **VERNON HOWARD**
with drawings by DOUG ANDERSON

STERLING PUBLISHING CO., Inc.   New York

ALSO BY THE SAME AUTHOR:

CONTENTS

I. Making Your Puppets

Puppets are just about the most interesting little people on earth! For thousands of years these lively performers have entertained and delighted audiences all over the world.

You too can build a fascinating puppet for yourself. You and your friends can put on puppet shows that will delight everyone, for you will have as much fun as your audiences! The following pages of this book will show you exactly how to do it.

There are dozens of kinds of puppets to choose from. In the next few paragraphs you will be shown how to create several different types. All of them are easy to make by using materials found in the home or schoolroom.

SOLID PUPPET: The head of this type of puppet is made from any solid object, such as an apple, potato, carrot, or perhaps a ball of tightly-packed newspaper. Almost any kind of solid object can serve as a head so long as you can scoop out a hole in the object. Make a channel large enough for your forefinger or for two fingers.

Next, turn your imagination loose to create a face. For example, you can make eyes out of colored thumbtacks and ears from pieces of cardboard. Make hair from strands of cotton or wool or from strips of paper and glue them to the head. Another way to make a face is to cover the head with a sock and then sew the features of the face onto the sock.

As a final step, drape a handkerchief over your hand and push your finger or fingers into the opening of the puppet-head. The handkerchief should be large enough to act as a coat or dress that covers your hand and arm. All puppets of this type need a coat or dress.

Your puppet is all ready to perform!

The solid puppet is one of the most popular among the many kinds of puppets. There are endless ways you can use this easy method to create different kinds of interesting little people.

Sock Puppet: You can turn an old sock into a puppet-person in just a few minutes. Stuff the end of the sock with newspaper or cotton to form the head. Sew on the face using buttons or pieces of cloth of contrasting colors, or paint on a face. Slip your hand into the open end of the sock and extend one or two fingers into the stuffed newspaper or cotton. By bending your fingers you can make your puppet move his head and upper body.

Socks are especially good for making animal puppets, such as a cat or a whale.

FRONT   BACK

STICK PUPPET: Few types of puppets are as easy to make as the kind we call stick puppets. You can make one by drawing a figure upon a piece of thick paper or thin cardboard. Cut the figure free from the rest of the paper. If your audience will be seeing both sides of the puppet you should dress or cover both sides of the figure. Paste your puppet-person to the end of a slender stick so that the stick serves as a handle. Make sure the stick is long enough so that the puppet can appear above the stage while your hand remains out of sight.

PAPER SACK PUPPET: A small or medium-size paper sack can turn into an interesting puppet-person. Draw a face on the sack, or paste on bits of paper to form the features. Cut a hole on each side of the sack, one for your thumb and one for your little finger. These are the arms of your puppet. If the sack is not long enough to cover your arm, paste on an extra piece of paper to serve as the rest of the coat or dress.

LEG PUPPET: Your own fingers will form the legs of this kind of puppet. He can actually walk and dance and hop merrily about the stage.

Draw a puppet-person on a piece of cardboard. Color the figure and cut it out. Make two holes at the place where the legs should go. Push your forefinger and your middle finger down through the holes as legs. Your leg puppet is ready to dance!

MOVING OBJECT: A moving object is any kind of a non-human and non-animal figure that moves while onstage. Here are some examples: train, boat, airplane, bicycle, balloon, kite, sun, moon, star, clouds, swaying building, rolling ball.

A moving object adds extra excitement to your puppet show. For instance, instead of having a puppet-person walk onto the stage you can build a cardboard automobile for him to ride in. As another example, you could build a stunt around a tall tree that sways back and forth and almost topples over in a storm. A moving object can be flat, with a stick attached as explained in the section on stick puppets, or can be made round, and worn over your hand.

Some objects move through the sky, such as an airplane or the sun. Attach such an object to a stick and hold it downward from the top of the stage.

Give your audience an extra treat by including moving objects in your puppet show!

YOUR PUPPET'S PERSONALITY

Your puppet will be especially appealing to both you and your audience if you give it a definite personality. This means that your puppet-person should have his own special character which is unlike any other performer on the stage.

The main idea is to make him an outstanding individual with his own mannerisms, with his special way of dressing, and with his particular way of walking and talking. For instance, he might be a *happy* and *lighthearted* type of person who laughs constantly, or he might be a puppet-person who is outstanding because of his *mighty muscles* or because he wears the *costume of a space-man*, or maybe he is noticeable because he is much *taller* than the rest of the puppets onstage.

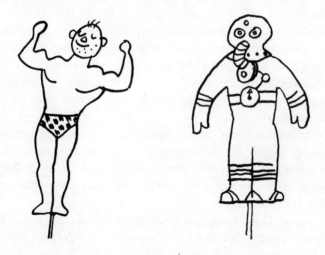

Use your puppet's costume to give him a special personality. Think of ways to dress him in an interesting style.

The facial features of your puppet will also help to make him outstanding in appearance. Remember to give him a face that attracts attention. The features of a puppet should be exaggerated. Give him an extra big nose or a very crooked mouth, so that the audience can recognize him easily.

Let your puppet speak and act according to the kind of a person he is. If he is supposed to be an excited and eager sort of person, have him talk and move around with enthusiasm. If he is in a sleepy mood, let him act as if he wants to go to bed.

The personality of your puppet is half the show! Show your audience an interesting personality!

PUPPETS IN ACTION

When putting on any kind of a show or stunt with puppets, keep your actions clear and simple. In some cases you can help your audience to understand the action by having the puppet speak aloud to himself as he goes about his act. For instance he might say, "I'll look under this tree for a place to sit."

When preparing your show, keep in mind the viewpoint of the audience. For example, if a puppet is going to bed, ask yourself how he should perform so that the action will be clear to the audience. Puppeteers can check each other during rehearsal to make sure that the movements are easy to understand.

To make sure that your audience can tell which puppet is speaking, jiggle the talking puppet somewhat as he talks. The talking puppet could also nod his head or move slightly forward. The other puppets onstage should remain motionless until their turn to speak.

Be sure that your puppet-person speaks clearly. Your audience wants and needs to know what he is saying. Remember it is harder to understand a person's voice when you can't watch his face and lips while he talks.

Do not hide one puppet behind another. Check this during rehearsal by having someone watch the act from the viewpoint of the audience.

When your show does not call for lots of onstage action from your puppets, you can include more puppet-people than when there is lots of movement. For instance, if you have a choral group which remains in one place and sings, you could use five or six puppets, or even more, depending upon the size of your stage.

Let your puppets exaggerate both their feelings and the actions that go with the feelings. An excited puppet should be wildly excited, while a tired puppet-man should groan and sag so wearily that the audience knows instantly how tired he is.

In a one-man show where the puppeteer operates behind a curtain, you can use several puppets. The puppeteer pulls one puppet offstage and then quickly comes back with another.

Some of the plays and stunts supplied in this book are just right for a single showman, while others can be presented by two or more puppeteers. The exact number of puppeteers and puppets can be decided upon before the play goes into rehearsal.

MAKING YOUR PUPPET THEATER

Your puppet theater can be as simple or as fancy as you like. The important idea is to make the theater and its stage suitable for the kind of show you are going to present. A show having several puppets needs a stage larger than one used for a one-man show. If your play includes flying birds, then your stage should have a screen at its top so that the puppeteers can remain hidden from the audience while holding their birds downward from the roof of the stage. It will not take you very long to plan the kind of theater that will best serve your show.

Here are several ways to build a puppet theater:

BLANKET THEATER: A blanket theater is excellent for presenting plays with a large cast of puppets. Make the stage as wide as necessary. As many as six or seven puppets, or even more, can perform onstage at the same time.

The theater consists of a blanket or sheet which is stretched out to any desired length across the room or yard. Fasten the ends to solid objects to hold the blanket up. Perhaps you can fasten the ends to a door or a window.

The puppeteers stand behind the blanket and hold their puppets above its top edge. The ample room behind the blanket makes it possible for several puppeteers to have their puppets onstage at the same time.

This type of theater is superb for outdoor use. Then you can suspend the blanket between posts or trees.

TABLE THEATER: Here the top of a table serves as your stage. Fasten a blanket or sheet over one side of the table and let it hang down as far as the floor. The purpose of the blanket is to hide you from the audience which sits in front of the table. You sit or kneel behind the table and hold your puppet up to perform on the table top.

Box Theater: This is a small theater which is good for one puppet or perhaps for a pair of performers. First of all, follow the instructions given above for making a *Table Theater*. Next, find an oblong box, such as an orange crate, and remove two of its sides. This leaves you with a frame consisting of the other two sides and the two ends. Place a blanket on top of the table (to prevent the box from scratching it), then set the box on its side on top of the blanket. Stand or sit in back of the table and let your puppets act inside the box.

Doorway Theater: Your stage will be as wide as the doorway you use. Fasten a blanket or sheet across a doorway so that its lower half is covered. Stand behind the blanket and hold your puppet above it.

WINDOW THEATER: Here is your ready-made showplace. Find a first-floor window that offers room on one side for your audience and space on the other side for the puppeteers. A porch window is often just right. Open the window, keep yourself below the sill, and hold your puppets up.

EXTRA IDEAS FOR EXTRA-GOOD SHOWS

In most cases the puppeteers will remain hidden behind the stage. However, a single puppeteer can perform in full view of the audience and without any stage at all. He can do this by holding the puppet away from him and turning his head away from the audience when the puppet is supposed to be speaking. He speaks to the puppet with one voice and answers with another. The puppet should wiggle around a bit when it is speaking. Also, the puppeteer can sit on a chair with the puppet on his knee.

If your stage has no curtain, the play can begin as the puppets come onstage for the first time. The puppets can end their act simply by bowing and leaving the stage. Another idea is for an assistant to flash a card reading THE END.

The teacher or director can introduce an act with a few words. First of all, it is nice to give the audience a cheery welcome to the theater. The introduction can then describe at least briefly the background of the act. For instance, "The play which you are about to see takes place at the seashore. Let's see what happens down among the sands and waves." A single performer can introduce his own act, or he can let the puppet speak!

You need very little scenery and stage properties for a puppet show. In many cases you can do without them altogether. However, it often adds to the showmanship of the play to set the stage with toy furniture and with small pictures on the wall.

Sound effects always add extra punch to a performance. Someone can be appointed to make the sounds that go with the onstage action. With very little equipment you can create sounds like storms and explosions and galloping horses. The sound effect should be timed correctly so that it is heard at exactly the same moment that the onstage action occurs.

In the language of the theater, the *right wing* means the wing to the right of the puppet as he stands onstage and faces the audience, while *left wing* is to the puppet's left. *Upstage* is to the rear of the stage, while *downstage* is toward the audience. Once you know stage directions, you are practically in show business!

2. How to Build
Your First Puppet Shows

The best way to learn to do something is to plunge right into it and perform the best you can. This not only helps you to learn new skills very rapidly but it gives you fun and adventure! You will win increasing confidence in your abilities to put on a lively show before an audience. Also, you will gain the general experience that will turn you into an expert puppeteer.

These first puppet plays will help you to learn the art of puppetry in an interesting manner. They will make you familiar with puppets, no matter what type of puppet you use. However, you will find that stick puppets are particularly good for group puppet shows. You can make large numbers of them quickly and easily, and a lot of them can fit on the stage at one time.

The plays in this section are especially easy to perform. They make good practice for any puppet group. They also give lots of pleasure—to both your audience and you!

ACT-AS-YOU-GO PUPPET PLAYS

These plays are called act-as-you-go because that is exactly how you perform them. You do not memorize words or actions; you simply make up the play as you go along. This is called an *impromptu* performance. An impromptu play is really easy to perform. Here are a few rules to help you:

a. Select one of the combinations of characters listed below. Choose one that appeals to you and make the puppets.

b. Get off by yourself, or with your partner if there are two of you in the play. Practice for a short time. Get to know your puppet characters.

c. When the play goes on, let your puppets speak and act in a natural manner. In other words, let the characters and the situations suggest ideas to you. Take, for example, the characters of the farmer and the crow. At the beginning of the play, it would be natural for the farmer to try to chase the crow out of his cornfield. Next, the crow might try to talk the farmer out of some free corn. The farmer might tell the crow that he must work for his food. The crow might object at first, but finally decide to earn his corn, so the farmer hands the crow a shovel. At the end of the play, both the farmer and the crow are happy with each other.

d. The most important thing to do with an act-as-you-go performance is to turn the puppets loose! Let them speak and act as they like. Let them enjoy themselves. That is how to make the play enjoyable for everyone!

1. A farmer and a crow.
2. A king and a queen.
3. Two jungle explorers.
4. A caveman and a dinosaur.
5. A pair of weathermen.
6. A witch and a goblin.
7. Two carpenters.
8. A pianist and a dancer.

9. A boy and his dog.
10. A butterfly and a bee.
11. Two detectives.
12. A knight-in-armor and a dragon.
13. Mother and daughter.
14. Two monkeys in a zoo.
15. A salesman and a customer.
16. A cowboy and his horse.
17. A pair of clowns.
18. A general and a private.
19. Two ghosts.
20. A bluebird and a blackbird.
21. A prince and a beautiful lady.
22. A polar bear and an Eskimo.
23. Two goldfish in a bowl.
24. A pair of cooks in a restaurant.
25. A girl and her pet kitten.
26. Two fishermen in a boat.
27. A pair of classmates.
28. A giant and a fairy.
29. A sailor and a whale.
30. Father and son.
31. Two men on a raft at sea.
32. A pair of elephants.
33. A girl and an owl.
34. Two football players.
35. A forest ranger and a squirrel.

PUPPETS IN ACTION

Here is a show put on by puppeteers for the benefit of puppeteers! Everyone can increase his skill by taking part.

The main idea is to learn about the many things your puppet can do while onstage, and to discover the dozens of different physical movements he is capable of doing. The more life you can put into your puppet-actor the more interesting he will be. And the more interesting he is, the more you will please your audience.

Each puppeteer thinks of two or three different movements for his puppet to perform. Each should be a clear-cut movement and a simple one. The puppeteer does not tell the others about the actions; he rehearses them by himself. The movements can consist of almost anything. Here are a few examples of a puppet in action:

1. He shakes wildly and laughs heartily.
2. He sways from side to side, walks dizzily, groans.
3. He trips over something and falls down with a yell.
4. He races around, glancing this way and that, as if excitedly searching for something.
5. He crosses the stage with only his head showing, as if walking in a trench.

The puppeteer sends his puppet-actor into a single action while the others watch. If the audience is unable to understand what the puppet is doing, the puppeteer can explain it.

After a puppeteer has performed just one of his several movements, he leaves the back of the stage and another takes his place. Later on, the first puppeteer comes back for a second or third turn. In this way everyone gains extra experience in entering and leaving the stage.

Just by watching the different actions of the others, a puppeteer adds to his own knowledge of what a puppet can do. And a puppet-person can do more than you may think!

SHORT SCENES

A series of short acts can make a fascinating puppet show. They are just right for those learning the art of puppetry. Here is how to build a show of short scenes:

Each puppeteer makes a puppet and prepares a single act which takes no more than a few seconds to perform. The puppets then appear onstage, one after another, until each has had his turn. This gives everyone an opportunity to practice his skills.

The teacher (or master of ceremonies) tells the audience that the curtain is about to rise upon a street scene. The teacher explains that all sorts of people will be coming down the street. Also, the teacher adds, these people will be fascinating to watch.

The curtain rises. The puppets come onstage, one at a time. They enter from either wing, perform their act, and exit at either wing.

With small groups of puppeteers, each person could take two or three turns across the stage.

Puppeteers can turn their imaginations loose to work up any kind of act they like. Or, they can use one of the following lively scenes:

1. A goat-puppet says to the audience, "I'm supposed to be a goat-puppet, but someone made a mistake in making me. Listen carefully and you'll see what I mean." As he exits he barks "woof-woof" like a dog.

2. A puppet tells a joke or a brief story.

3. The puppet enters laughing loudly. He explains to the audience, "I'm practicing to be a laughing clown."

4. A puppet rides across the stage while mounted upon a cardboard elephant.

5. The puppet walks to the center of the stage and explains to the audience, "The only thing I have learned to do so far is to walk. So I'll walk for you." He walks offstage.

6. A puppet jumps back and forth across the stage. He finally flies out the left wing, and a moment later a loud crash is heard.

7. The puppet sails across the stage in a cardboard boat.

8. The puppet enters bent over as if searching the ground. He looks up to the audience and says, "I'm looking for a puppet show. I can't seem to find one anywhere. Oh, well, I'll keep looking." He exits while searching.

9. A puppet recites a short poem.

10. The puppet faces the audience and announces, "I'm learning how to be invisible. You know what invisible means— it means you can't see me. So the next time you see nothing on this stage—that will be me!"

11. A bird-puppet flies back and forth a few times while dipping and soaring.

12. A puppet sings as he crosses. He explains to the audience, "I may not have much of a voice, but I do have the courage to try." He exits while singing.

13. A witch rides around on a broom while shrieking.

14. A monkey-puppet hops onstage to tell the audience, "I'm sorry I don't have time to put on a show for you, but I'm busy looking for some peanuts. If you see any, please let me know." He hops offstage.

15. The puppets asks a riddle and supplies the answer.

16. A potato-puppet enters and says to the audience, "I am

a potato. I can talk. If you have never heard a talking potato before, you are hearing one now. See you later." He bows and leaves.

17. A lion-puppet crosses while roaring at the audience.

18. A puppet rushes onstage, shouting and jumping noisily. He suddenly stops and faces the audience to remark, "What a noisy puppet *I* am!" He noisily exits.

19. The puppet drives across the stage in a cardboard automobile.

20. A boy-puppet leans forward toward the audience to say, "Hello, Mary Lou. Are you out there, Mary Lou? Nice to see you, Mary Lou." The puppet straightens up and tells the audience, "It's a funny thing, but I don't even know a girl named Mary Lou." He exits with a shrug.

21. A fish-puppet swims lazily around for a few seconds.

22. A puppet dressed as a king enters and speaks to the audience in a sad voice, "I am a king. But I have a problem. I have no country to be the king of. A king has to have a country if he is to be a king at all. So if you will excuse me, I have to look for a country to be king of." He exits.

23. A pumpkin-puppet enters and explains to the audience, "I'm practicing for Hallowe'en."

24. A soldier-puppet marches onstage. He goes through the actions of a real soldier on parade and finally marches off.

25. A girl-puppet enters carrying a flower twice as big as herself. She cheerfully tells the audience, "This is what happens when you water your flower garden every day!"

ACTING CONTEST

An acting contest for puppets is more than fun. It helps to build superior shows. It is always helpful to watch the way other puppeteers perform.

The contest starts as the teacher or leader assigns everyone the same act, no matter what kind of puppets they have made. For instance, each puppeteer (or puppeteer partners) could be assigned to act out the role of nature hikers. One after another, the puppets come onstage for a minute or two and perform their act. A nature hiker could pretend to find a dove's feather; he could exclaim in wonderment at a beautiful sunset; he could act out just about anything that a nature hiker would come across.

As each act is performed, the puppeteers in the audience should study them, noticing both strong and weak points. The whole idea is for each puppeteer to improve his own act by watching the acts of others. The teacher could lead a discussion about the various acts in order to discover ways to make them more interesting.

When all the acts are finished, the puppeteers vote for the performance which they liked best. A small prize might be awarded to the winner or winners. Even some enthusiastic applause is a good prize! But everyone really wins in a puppet contest, for it helps to turn out better acts.

RHYMING PUPPETS

Writing the dialogue for puppet plays can be lots of fun all by itself. One of the cleverest ways to write a script for your show is to make up simple rhymes for a pair of puppets to speak.

You can start off by writing down pairs of words that rhyme, such as *gate* and *late; pig* and *fig; song* and *long.*

Next, build a two-line poem from each pair of rhyming words. Here are examples of how they might come out:

> *Why are you late?*
> *I was stuck in the gate.*

> *I see a pig.*
> *Go feed it a fig.*

> *Sing me a song.*
> *A short one or long?*

A pair of puppeteers can write six or seven of these rhymes and speak them one after another. One puppet speaks the first line and his partner the second.

To help remember the lines, write them down on a sheet of paper and pin it to the back of the stage.

COSTUME CONTEST

The preparation of a puppet show should be filled with as much fun as possible. One way to rehearse and have fun at the same time is to stage a costume contest.

The teacher or leader of the group announces that a costume contest will be held before the show is performed for a real audience. This gives the puppeteers time to think about and work with the costumes for their puppets.

When everyone has clothed his puppet, the contest is staged. Each puppet appears onstage for a few seconds, long enough for the audience of puppeteers to get a good look at him. The onstage puppet can say a few words about himself, or he can perform a simple stunt, such as hopping about.

The puppeteers vote for the best costumes. It is a good idea to offer two prizes—one for the cleverest costume and one for the funniest or strangest.

You can make attractive costumes from dozens of materials which are easy to obtain. Here are a few suggestions: old clothing, colored paper, newspaper, cardboard, cotton, aluminum foil, string, yarn, ribbons, beads, buttons, flowers, leaves, twigs, berries.

SECRET VOICES

A skillful puppeteer has many secret voices. He can make his puppet shriek like a witch or roar like a lion or speak with the squeaky voice of an elf. When you give your puppet a special voice you can make him twice as interesting!

Here is how you and your puppeteer friends can play a game while learning to develop secret voices:

Each puppeteer finds a partner. They get together and decide on two kinds of voices to use, say the voice of Santa Claus and that of a dog. They then have a conversation, using their secret voices. The audience, which is made of up other puppeteers, tries to guess who the voices represent.

The puppeteers should try to include sounds which are natural to the person or animal they are imitating. For instance, Santa Claus would laugh heartily and the dog might growl and bark as he speaks. If the audience is unable to guess correctly, the puppets can speak lines that will make it easier. Santa Claus could ask the dog what he wants for Christmas, and the dog might ask for a fresh bone.

Here are twelve voices which can be used for practice:

1. A seal.
2. A witch.
3. A crow.
4. A lion.
5. A small child.
6. An excited person.
7. A cat.
8. A goat.
9. A sleepy person.
10. An elf.
11. A parrot.
12. A mixed-up person.

BUILDING A PLAY THE EASY WAY

Once you have an idea to start you off, you can easily work out a play. Listed below you will find fifty good background ideas which can form the central themes of your puppet plays. Here is how to use them to create a puppet play of your own, quickly and simply:

a. Select a background that you like.

b. Add some characters suitable to the background.

c. Plan some actions that connect the characters with their background.

Once you have taken these three steps you will be delighted at how easily the play develops itself. It is almost as if the puppet-people themselves know just what to say and do!

Let's take an example. Suppose you select the background of a farm. What characters would be suitable to such a background? Let's choose a farmer, his horse, his cow and a frog.

The next question is, how can we get our four puppet-characters to act in a way that tells some sort of a story? Well, maybe the frog makes so much noise at night that the horse and the cow cannot sleep. They complain to the farmer, who suggests that they all go down and have a talk with the frog. They do, but the frog has his own complaint. He says that *he* cannot sleep during the day because of the horse's whinny and the cow's moo. The problem is solved as everyone agrees to be more understanding and forgiving of the natural habits of others. All four characters sing a cheery song together as the curtain falls on a happy ending.

That is one way to build lively puppet plays the easy way. Try it for yourself and you will find how much fun play-making can be.

1. On a farm.
2. In a castle.
3. At the seashore.
4. In a bakery.
5. On an island.
6. In a hat shop.
7. At a banquet.
8. In the woods.
9. At a circus.
10. In the kitchen.
11. At a playground.
12. In a lighthouse.
13. In a vegetable garden.
14. At a picnic.
15. In a planetarium.
16. On the ocean floor.
17. In a storm.
18. In a pickle factory.
19. On the front porch.
20. In a grocery market.
21. In an elevator.
22. On the moon.
23. In a ranger station.

24. At a zoo.
25. In a cave.
26. In the desert.
27. In a museum.
28. On a ranch.
29. In the snow.
30. In the attic.
31. In a submarine.
32. At a flower shop.
33. In a space rocket.
34. On a river bank.
35. In a fire station.
36. At the library.
37. In a cornfield.
38. On a mountain-top.
39. In a schoolroom.
40. In an airplane.
41. At a beauty shop.
42. In a business office.
43. On a train.
44. At an ice cream factory.
45. In an apple orchard.
46. At an army camp.
47. In a science laboratory.
48. At a club meeting.
49. At the post office.
50. In a newspaper office.

3.   Exciting Puppet Plays

Here are some highly entertaining puppet plays in which the basic actions and words are supplied for you. Each play is given in twelve simple steps. By following the directions you can quickly and easily build an exciting show.

The twelve steps are ready for your immediate rehearsal. You will find that your practice sessions help you to add your own special ideas to the performance. Do not hesitate to include any good ideas that may occur to you. Everyone presents a play in a somewhat different manner, so keep adding your own special touch to the show. For instance, you may think up some plans for including sound effects.

As you practice the play, remember to include some of the suggestions listed in the first pages of this book. They can often make the difference between an average and a superior performance.

Some of these plays are excellent for large casts of four or more puppets. Others are more suitable for a smaller number of actors. A *Blanket Theater* is best for a large number of puppet-performers.

THE LIGHTHOUSE

1. Inside the lighthouse, the two lighthouse-keepers move around, attending to their work. One of them, named Tom, steps forward and looks out and over the heads of the audience while saying, "A storm is coming up, Sam. The ships may need some help. Don't you think we ought to turn on the big spotlight?"

2. Without bothering to look up, Sam shakes his head and replies, "Not yet, Tom. The ships are all right."

3. Two cardboard ships sail in from opposite wings. They dip and sway, as if in a somewhat rough sea. They pass each other and exit.

4. The puppets resume their work, chatting and humming.

5. Tom again looks over the heads of the audience. He shakes his head worriedly and says, "It's a storm all right. Maybe we ought to turn on the big spotlight."

6. Sam chuckles and replies confidently as he continues to work, "Not yet, Tom. The ships can see where they're going."

7. The two cardboard ships again sail onstage. They shake more violently than before, as if the storm has increased. They pass and exit.

8. The puppets once more work around the lighthouse for a few moments. Tom steps downstage and worriedly peers out. He changes his position and looks again. He shakes his head and says, "Sam, don't you think we should turn on the big spotlight? It's getting rough out there."

9. Without looking up, Sam laughs, "No, no. Don't worry about it. The ships are perfectly safe."

10. Sam continues to work, while Tom worriedly paces back and forth while peering outward. Tom suddenly shrieks, "Sam, look! Please turn on the big spotlight! Look out there!"

11. Sam laughs and continues to work. As Tom watches, the two ships enter while twisting and shaking as if in a violent storm. As they meet, both sink slowly downward and out of sight.

12. Sam looks up and laughs, "Well, since you are so worried, I'll just go out and turn on the big spotlight." He chuckles, exits, returns a second later and laughs at Tom, "All right, the big spotlight is turned on. Do you feel better now?" As he speaks, the two ships rise slowly, continue to cross, and exit while shaking violently. Tom sighs, "I'm sure glad we turned on that big spotlight." The curtain falls.

THE TREASURE HUNTERS

1. The treasure hunters bounce merrily onstage. They carry cardboard picks and shovels; one carries a large map.

2. They talk excitedly about buried treasure. They remark that it was hidden by pirates, that it is probably worth millions of dollars, and so on.

3. The puppet with the map calls out, "According to this map we are standing right over the treasure!" They all yell, "Let's start digging!"

4. They dig furiously, while yelling excitedly. They gradually sink deeper and deeper until the audience can see only their upper parts.

5. As they dig, bits of colored paper—representing earth and stones—fly upward.

6. They climb wearily upward until they are in full view once more. They peer downward into the pit and make complaining remarks, such as, "I'm getting tired," and, "I wonder how much deeper we have to dig?"

7. One of them says, "Let's get back to work." Another replies, "Let's go!" They dive completely out of sight, come half way up, again dig and shout furiously.

8. They repeat the action of points 6 and 7.

9. They gradually disappear until only the tops of their heads can be seen by the audience. Their heads jerk back and forth as they dig and yell.

10. They finally disappear downward altogether. The colored paper continues to fly upward.

11. They shoot upward into view, yelling with delight. As they look downward into their pit they call out, "There it is!" and, "I wonder what kind of treasure we have?"

12. They dive downward out of sight. For a moment or two there is total silence. They then climb upward into view. They hold up a large bone for the audience to see and remark, "A dog bone!" and "Well, it would be a treasure for some hungry hound." They merrily bounce offstage.

THE WRESTLERS

1. One of the wrestlers appears onstage from right wing. The other appears at left.

2. They eye each other, growl, and stir their feet around as they get ready to rush at each other.

3. They yell, rush at each other, miss completely, pass by each other and crash offstage.

4. They reappear, sway groggily about for a few seconds, again growl at each other.

5. Again they yell and speed toward each other. They hit head-on, bounce back violently and fly offstage with another crash.

6. They reappear, rush at each other, and wrestle.

7. One wrestler throws the other offstage. The other returns and throws his opponent offstage.

8. They wrestle furiously, shrieking and groaning.

9. With swift movements they repeat the action of rushing at each other, missing, and ending up in an offstage crash.

10. They rush at each other several times, knocking each other in various directions.

11. They wrestle some more, but both grow slow and tired. They fall together to the floor where they lie in silence for a moment or two.

12. They rise together. One invites the other, "Let's be friends." The other replies, "It's much better to be friends." Arm in arm they exit happily.

THE SINGING DRAGON

1. The children race around the woods, laughing and shouting. They make happy remarks about the birds and flowers.

2. As they play, a singing voice is heard. As it grows closer and louder, the children stop to listen. One of them asks, "What's that?" Another replies, "It must be a happy hunter."

3. As they look into the right wing, they gasp in fright. One of them shouts in alarm, "Look! It's a dragon!" Another cries out, "Let's hide!" They rush upstage and hide by crouching.

4. The dragon enters with a dance step, singing merrily. He does not notice the children as he waltzes around the stage. Suddenly he halts, faces the audience and says, "I think I hear some children hiding. It isn't easy to hear children when they are hiding, but I think I hear some children hiding. I'd better have a look."

5. The dragon searches about while singing and dancing. As he finally sees the crouching children, he cheerfully greets them. "Good morning, hiding children. I am a dragon. I am a singing dragon. Want to hear me sing?" He sings a few notes.

6. The children step forward with curiosity. One of them says, "I never heard of a *singing* dragon. I don't think you are really a dragon." Another child adds, "A dragon is supposed to roar like thunder and shoot fire from his mouth."

7. The dragon is deeply hurt. He sniffs, "Well, all right, I'll try to roar it for you, but I'm out of practice." He tries to roar but it comes out faint and weak.

8. The children shake their heads and remark that there is no such thing as a *singing* dragon. They agree that he must be an *un*dragon.

9. The children start to leave at the left wing. One of them waves to the dragon and says, "Good-by, Mister *Un*dragon." The children exit at left.

10. The dragon weeps, groans and rolls on the ground. As he does so, the children re-enter. One of them says, "Maybe we should have believed him." Another child adds, "I guess he's a real dragon after all."

11. The children give the dragon some comforting pats. One child says, "We believe you, Mr. Dragon. We thought that all dragons had to roar and shoot fire. A dragon can be a *singing* dragon if he wants. Go ahead and sing. We like you to be a singing dragon."

12. The dragon happily sings a familiar song. The children gather around him and join in the singing. The curtain falls.

CANDY COUNTER

1. The candy clerk stands behind the counter and happily remarks that he sees customers coming his way.

2. The children rush in. The clerk asks them what kind of candy they want. They all call out for chocolates.

3. The clerk hands out chocolates, which the children pay for.

4. The children hungrily eat their chocolates while remarking how delicious they are.

5. One child asks the others what kind of candy to buy next. They discuss it and agree on peppermints.

6. The children call out for peppermints. The clerk asks them how they can still eat more candy, but sells them the peppermints.

7. The children eat the peppermints with less enthusiasm than they ate the chocolates. One or two of them groan.

8. One child asks the others what kind of candy they should buy next. Without enthusiasm they agree to try some taffy.

9. They ask the clerk for some taffy. He shakes his head and warns them against more candy, but sells them the taffy.

10. The children force themselves to eat the taffy, while groaning and staggering around the stage.

11. One child tells the others that it is time for them to go on to the contest. The clerk asks them what contest they are talking about. A child tells him that it is a candy-eating contest.

12. As the children moan and exit, a child explains to the clerk that they were practicing for a candy-eating contest.

SLEEPYTIME

1. The stage is divided into two bedrooms which are separated by a cardboard wall that runs down the center of the stage from upstage to downstage. A puppet enters sleepily from the right wing. He stretches, groans sleepily, and climbs into bed. He dozes peacefully.

2. A second puppet races onstage from the left. He shouts, leaps about, jumps up and down, and makes cheery noises of all sorts.

3. The sleepy puppet jerks up, leaps out of bed, races frantically around the room in an effort to find the source of the noise. He mutters in annoyance at the disturbance.

4. The noisy puppet suddenly becomes silent, so the sleepy puppet wearily goes back to bed and tries to sleep.

5. The noisy puppet walks around quietly for a moment, then remarks, "It's too quiet in here." Suddenly he breaks out with another series of shouts and leaps. The sleepy puppet again jumps from his bed and runs around while frantically complaining.

6. The noisy puppet rushes offstage at left and the noise ceases. The sleepy puppet stretches, groans, and staggers back to bed. He dozes peacefully for a few seconds.

7. The noisy puppet again races in, yelling and bouncing around. The sleepy puppet shoots out of bed and pounds his head against the wall repeatedly. He yells, "Quiet, quiet, quiet! I'm trying to sleep! Quiet!"

8. The noisy puppet quiets down. He walks softly around the room for a moment, groans wearily and goes to bed.

9. The sleepy puppet turns and tosses, unable to sleep. He finally gets up and paces the floor while groaning, "I can't sleep, I can't sleep. All that noise next door keeps me awake. I just can't sleep."

10. The sleepy puppet paces the floor for a while, then finally exclaims, "I've got a bright idea—a very bright idea!"

He goes to the wall, pounds it with his head and calls out, "Hello! Hello, next door! Are you awake? I've got a good idea!"

11. The noisy puppet gets up, speaks back through the wall, "What's your bright idea?" The sleepy puppet replies, "Come on over and I'll tell you."

12. The noisy puppet exits at left and enters the other bedroom by coming in at the right wing. The sleepy puppet says to him, "Since neither of us can sleep, I've got a bright idea. Let's both make noise!" The noisy puppet yells, "Great idea!" and races back to his own room. Both puppets yell and jump around for awhile. Finally, both stretch sleepily and stagger into bed. They fall asleep and the curtain closes.

EXERCISE

1. The athletic coach bounces into the gym. He calls out, "Time to exercise!" and performs a few comical twists and turns while counting aloud, "One-two-three-four, one-two-three-four."

2. The class enters, walking slowly and with droopy posture. The class greets the coach without enthusiasm. He tells them sternly to go out and come back in with some energy. The class exits slowly, then returns a second later by zooming speedily onstage.

3. The coach informs the class that it is time for morning exercise. As they line up, he leads them in jumping up and down a few times.

4. The coach calls for a backward bend. They perform this exercise by bending backward until their heads touch the floor. As they bend back and forth the coach cheerfully remarks, "I'd like to see a human being do that!"

5. The coach next calls for some running exercises, so the puppets race around the stage. The coach calls out, "One-two-three-four, one-two-three-four."

6. The puppets slow down as they get tired of running. The coach urges them on. Finally, as the class is about to collapse from exhaustion, the coach calls a halt.

7. As the class sags and puffs, the coach says, "All right. You can have a short rest." The puppets collapse on the floor. A second later the coach yells, "Time to go! On your feet! Everyone up!"

8. They rise and exercise back and forth by bending sideways until they are flat on the stage; they then straighten up and bend sideways to the other side. The coach counts aloud.

9. The coach yells into a wing, calling for a ball. A ball or balloon rolls onstage. The class kicks and knocks it around for awhile. An offstage assistant sees that it stays onstage.

10. The coach announces that he is going out for a drink of water. He says that upon his return the class will do some more running exercises. He leaves them with the remark, "Get ready to run!"

11. While the coach is offstage, the puppets rush together at stage center. They get their heads close together and whisper excitedly.

12. The coach returns and yells, "Everyone run! One-two-three-four!" The puppets run around for a moment, then run offstage one by one, until the stage is empty. The coach remarks, "Well, I guess I *did* tell them to run! I might as well run myself." He runs offstage while counting aloud.

THE COSTUME PARTY

1. One by one the guests arrive at the party. They are greeted by the host or hostess. All guests are in costume, one or two as animals.

2. The guests mingle and chat.

3. The host announces that they will have a singing session. Everyone harmonizes in singing a familiar song or two.

4. Music is played. Everyone dances.

5. The host announces that they will play Hide and Seek. While the others turn their backs and count aloud, one of the guests hides by huddling in an upstage corner. The seekers rush around, offstage and back, trying to find him. As they give up and stand together downstage, the hider creeps up from behind and yells out. They leap in surprise.

6. Refreshments are served. The guests dine and drink.

7. One of the guests does a comical dance. As he finishes, the others applaud.

8. A guest tells a joke. The others laugh.

9. The host asks one of the guests to do an imitation. The guest imitates an animal. The others applaud.

10. The host invites everyone to have fun. The guests leap about, wrestle, run offstage and back, and have a wild time in general.

11. The guests remark that it is time to go. One by one they thank the host and exit.

12. As the last guest leaves, the host turns to the audience and thanks everyone for coming to the party. The host exits and the curtain falls.

FOOTBALL FANS

1. The spectators at a football stadium come onstage while excitedly chatting about the forthcoming game.

2. As the game starts, they cheer loudly for their team.

3. They fall all over each other in frenzied excitement as their team scores.

4. The spectators cheer in unison, as a yell.

5. As their team fumbles the ball, they roll all over the stage while groaning and making gloomy remarks.

6. A hot dog vendor enters, spills his tray all over the protesting spectators.

7. An absent-minded spectator cheers loudly for the opposite team. As the others crowd around him with threatening glares, he again cheers the original team.

8. The spectators look upward while yelling that the football is sailing into the stands. As an offstage assistant tosses a toy ball onto the stage, the spectators scramble to catch it.

9. A spectator excuses himself several times, saying he needs a drink of water. He bumps into the others as he awkwardly exits and enters. They yell at him to sit down.

10. A spectator stretches and announces how tired he is. As he sleeps, the others try to arouse him with shakes and shouts, but without success. Another spectator then falls asleep; the others try to awaken him also. One by one, all fall asleep. All suddenly awaken in unison to cheer explosively for their team.

11. As their team wins, the spectators waltz around with each other.

12. While remarking about the tough game they had, the spectators drag themselves offstage wearily.

THE RUNNERS

1. Two or three runners enter from the right wing. They puff and stagger as if running a cross-country race.

2. In a series of actions they pass each other, fall behind each other, pass once more.

3. As they continue to pass and fall behind they yell out, loudly, "Wait for me!" and "Not so fast!" and "Here I come!"

4. The runners exit at the left wing, one after another. When they reappear at the right wing, they are in another order. This can be repeated several times throughout the play.

5. With odd and funny actions, the runners appear, cross the stage, disappear, and reappear. Here are a few examples: They run upside down. They flash back and forth as rapidly as the puppeteer's arm can move. They run into each other, collide, fall, and run once more.

6. The runners disappear at the left wing. When they reappear at right, one of the puppets is riding the shoulders of another. The next time across, the rider becomes the carrier.

7. The runner in front suddenly turns around and calls out, "Halt!" He then hands candy bars to the others, inviting,

"Here, have some candy." While the others munch their candy, the leading runner speeds offstage. The others suddenly wake up, yell out, speed offstage after him.

8. The puppets halt suddenly and peer into the left wing. They yell that they are approaching the finish line with, "There's the finish line!" and "We're almost there!"

9. They repeat the wild antics mentioned at Step 5 above. They finally disappear into the left wing.

10. The stage is empty for a moment. Then, all puppets appear from right wing. They wearily stumble to the center of the stage where they line up. The middle puppet says to the audience, "Sorry, we made a mistake. That wasn't the finish after all." Another puppet adds sadly, "It was just the beginning." The third puppet remarks, "So if you will excuse us, we have to be running!"

11. All puppets dash wildly around, repeating several of the previously listed actions.

12. All finally rush offstage as the curtain falls.

THE SCHOOL FOR SINGERS

1. The professor of the school for singers enters while singing off-key. He glances at his watch and remarks that it is time for his pupils to arrive.

2. One by one the pupils enter. They sing a happy greeting to the professor. He sings back a welcome.

3. The professor announces that practice will now begin. He leads them in singing the scale a few times.

4. A pupil requests that they be allowed to practice with a song. The professor agrees, then leads them in any familiar song, perhaps *Dixie* or *Sailing, Sailing*.

5. The pupils sing off-key and out of rhythm. The professor screams in dismay and rushes about in distress.

6. They sing the same song again, with the same off-key results.

7. The professor states that he will discover who is singing off-key. One by one he tests the pupils. All of them sing poorly. The professor rolls on the floor and groans.

8. The professor tells two of the pupils that he wants them to sing lower. They crouch down and sing briefly. He shouts that that was not what he meant.

9. The professor says that he will show them how to sing beautifully. He steps forward to the center of the stage and sings sourly while gesturing wildly. He then tells the pupils that *that* is what he wants to hear. The pupils now sing as did the professor, with sour notes and wild gestures. The professor nods in pleasure and says that they are doing much better.

10. The pupils and the professor jump excitedly up and down as they sing a fast and lively song.

11. The professor tells the pupils that they will now sing a special song for the audience.

12. The pupils sing a familiar tune, singing in harmony. All puppets bow and exit.

4. Special Fun
with Puppets

Puppets can perform so many exciting acts! They can entertain audiences in so many interesting ways!

This section will show you how to use your puppets in special ways for special fun. You will discover ideas for making your puppets dance. You will find the best way to build a comical puppet show. You will learn how to perform the kind of stunts that win enthusiastic applause from your audiences.

Some of the acts in this section run for just a minute or two. Some you can build into a performance that remains onstage for three or four minutes. You can choose the ones that run for the length of time you desire.

You can also use this material to present a variety show. Build up several short acts and then bring them onstage, one after another, with a short intermission between the acts.

"IT HAPPENED TO ME"

To build this stunt the puppeteer thinks of something that happened to him. It can be anything exciting or funny or just plain interesting. The puppeteer then sends his puppet onstage to act out the event. As the puppet acts, the puppeteer narrates. That is, he explains the action as it goes along.

Suppose your puppet is showing how he learned to swim. He could perform and explain all sorts of actions. He could start off by showing how he shivered when first touching the chilly water. Next, he could act out his first dive—an awkward leap which ends with a thud on the stage floor.

You can also make your puppet swim comically along. Just move him slowly across the stage while dipping him up and down. Let his head appear above the stage floor and then disappear below it as he swims.

Here are fifteen good ideas. They are typical of the kind that make good solo acts.

1. Learning to swim.
2. Searching for a lost object.
3. Cooking dinner.
4. Repairing a bicycle.
5. Hiking through the woods.
6. Trying to study in a noisy room.
7. Playing baseball.
8. Walking to school in a heavy rain.
9. Washing dishes.
10. Learning to dance.
11. Fishing from a rowboat.
12. Building a tree house.
13. Watching an exciting television show.
14. Shopping in a busy market.
15. Learning to play a musical instrument.

DANCING PUPPETS

Puppets which dance bouncily around the stage can put on an attractive and amusing show. Very little practice is needed to make the puppet-dancers move about in unison with music. Here are ten ideas for making the most of your dancing puppets:

1. Have a pair of puppets dance together, perhaps with a waltz.

2. Several puppeteers can take part by having some of the dancers exit as others enter.

3. In rhythm with exciting music, have a puppet or two perform a comical dance. They can leap, hop, dart across the stage, exit at the left wing and re-enter at the right.

4. Have the puppets sing as they dance.

5. The dancers can wear costumes of foreign lands.

6. Have a girl puppet dance gracefully about in harmony with soft music.

7. Have odd combinations of animals dancing as partners, such as a lion and a deer.

8. Change the pace of the dancing by speeding up or slowing down the music.

9. Build a short scene in which a girl teaches a boy to dance. At first he dances awkwardly, but grows increasingly skillful.

10. Finish your show of dancing puppets by having them dance offstage as the music concludes.

ANIMAL STUNT

This is a humorous stunt which can be a popular part of your puppet show. Since the puppets occupy only a small portion of the stage, as many as six or seven animal-puppets can take part.

Each puppeteer makes a puppet of an animal or a bird. Since this is a brief stunt, it is best to make stick puppets, for you can create one in just a few minutes. The puppeteer draws a picture of an animal or a bird (or clips a colored picture from an old magazine) and mounts it on a stick. The puppet should not be too large.

The show begins as one of the smaller puppets comes onstage while making appropriate animal sounds. For example, a cat could enter while *meowing*. Next, a somewhat larger animal enters and performs. For instance, a dog could run onstage while barking. One at a time the animals and birds continue to appear until the stage and the space above the stage is thick with puppets—all of them making their natural noises. The creatures run or fly about as best they can within their own small portion of the stage.

All the puppeteers watch for a signal from the teacher. At her signal everyone swiftly—and at the same time—pulls his puppet from the stage and becomes silent. When done in unison, this makes an interesting finish to the stunt.

SINGING PUPPETS

Puppets can be merry singers! Anyone can sing well enough to make his puppet sound interesting and amusing. Audiences always enjoy musical selections. For these three reasons, use the following ideas for adding extra showmanship to your puppet plays:

1. While working up a performance, find a place or two where you can include a song. Use songs that fit in with the play, like *Yankee Doodle* in a scene with a background of American history.

2. Let your puppets act out the playing of musical instruments as they sing along. It is easy to make small drums and horns. You can play real music offstage, or use a phonograph.

3. Let the puppets lead the audience in the singing of popular tunes.

4. Have the puppets march around the stage as they sing lively songs.

5. As one of the characters in a play, have someone who bursts into song every once in awhile.

6. Play a phonograph record with a solo singing voice. Let a puppet pretend to sing. You can also play a chorus of voices, while having several puppets onstage.

7. To make it appear as if a single puppet has several voices, have only one puppet onstage while several hidden voices sing.

8. Turn interesting puppet-characters into singers. Examples: a giant, a tiger, an alligator.

9. As background music to a pantomime play, have a hidden chorus sing softly.

10. Build a complete show around singing puppets. Have several acts, some of them humorous and others of a more serious nature.

PUPPETS FROM MANY LANDS

Puppet acts that take place in a foreign land are always welcome. It is easy to dress your puppets in a costume of another country, and just as easy to work up some actions for them to perform.

First of all, select one of the countries listed below. All of them are familiar lands which offer good opportunities for costumes and customs.

Next, build an act around some typical or colorful custom of the country. If you choose Switzerland you could show Swiss children playing in the snow of the Alps mountains. For a show taking place in Japan, your characters could cross a Japanese-style bridge over to an orchard of cherry blossoms.

1. Holland	6. India
2. Egypt	7. Japan
3. China	8. Italy
4. Spain	9. Ireland
5. Switzerland	10. Mexico

YOU ARE THE STAR

In this show, you are both the puppeteer and the puppet! The idea is for you and your friends to play yourselves. The puppet does not have to look exactly like you, but you can dress it in the same kind of clothing that you often wear.

You can build the play around one of the other ideas found in this book. For instance, in the play called *The Singing Dragon* on page 38 you and your friends could play the roles of the children. The main idea is for you to play yourself, whatever the play.

Another way to use this idea is for you and one or two friends to act out a scene based on your shared activities. Think of something that you do together, such as walking home from school. Ideas for dialogue and action will come very quickly once you start with a familiar activity.

It is important that the audience knows that you are playing yourself. This is best done just before the curtain rises. The teacher announces each person by name. Your puppet-self then appears onstage for a bow. When everyone has been introduced, the play begins. To help the audience remember, the puppets address each other by name—the puppeteers' name of course—frequently.

PERFORMING PUPPETS

This stunt is always good for a few minutes of fun at a puppet show and it usually produces some extra laughs. The announcer tells the audience that some of the puppets have been trained to obey any orders that anyone cares to give them. He invites members of the audience to command the puppets to perform.

The announcer stands aside as two or three puppets bounce onstage and bow. The audience then commands them to perform whatever stunts come to mind. The audience can ask them to run in a circle, to bump into each other, or sing a song. Half the fun of this stunt is that the audience will ask the puppets to do difficult or strange things. When the puppets try to obey the commands, the fun begins!

FUNNY PUPPETS

Puppets are natural comedians. They like nothing better than to have fun onstage. They can make the audience laugh, too. Here are ten good ideas for building comedy shows:

1. Dress your puppets in comic costumes, such as that of a clown and a scarecrow.

2. Have a puppet-character tell about something funny that happened to him. Let him go through funny motions as he tells his story.

3. Remember that your puppets can perform some amazing stunts. Turn them loose. Let them dart back and forth swiftly. Have a puppet disappear into one wing and reappear almost instantly at the opposite wing. Let a puppet hang downward from the ceiling. As you practice, you will think of many more funny stunts.

4. Build funny dialogues by using jokes. The puppeteers can search books and magazines for jokes that can be added to a comical conversation.

5. Put on a humorous dancing act. The puppets can whirl and fly about the stage.

6. Have a puppet-man who bursts into laughter all the time.

7. Have a puppet-girl who giggles constantly.

8. Make one of your puppet-characters an awkward sort of person who is always bumping into people and dropping things.

9. Speak with funny voices. Examples: a squeaky voice, a voice that sings its words, a shouting voice.

10. Give your comic characters interesting mannerisms. For instance, a puppet could bounce across the stage, instead of walking. Another character could always be eating something. A third puppet could have the habit of walking backwards, explaining that he likes to see where he has been.

QUESTION PUPPETS

This idea gets the audience into the act. It also gives acting experience to the puppeteer. The puppet comes onstage and asks any kind of an interesting question for the audience to guess. If the audience comes up with the right answer, the puppeteer goes on to another question. If the listeners fail to come up with a correct answer, the puppeteer supplies it.

Each puppet can ask three or four questions. The quizzes should not be too difficult, nor too easy. The following ten are good examples of the kind that can make an exciting quiz-show.

1. Who is Henry Wadsworth Longfellow? (an American poet).

2. In what country is the city of Tokyo? (Japan).

3. What is the Mona Lisa? (a famous painting).

4. On what continent do gorillas live in the jungle? (Africa).

5. The picture of what man is on a five-dollar bill? (Abraham Lincoln).

6. The name of what planet begins with the letter v? (Venus).

7. What are the first names of the Wright Brothers? (Orville and Wilbur).

8. On what continent is the country of Bolivia? (South America).

9. The name of what precious stone begins with the letter e? (emerald).

10. What state of the union is directly north of California? (Oregon).

SALESMAN AND CUSTOMER

Just get a salesman and a customer together! That is all you need for building a one-man show that includes two puppets.

The first thing to do is to build a pair of interesting puppet-characters, one as the salesman and the other for the customer. Choose two characters who are unlike each other in appearance and manner. For instance, the salesman could be a talkative and brash sort of person, while the customer is shy and never finishes a sentence. Or, it could be the other way around, with the customer loudly demanding faster and better service from a meek and nervous clerk.

Next, decide upon the type of product which the customer is seeking to buy. It can be almost anything from an automobile to a pair of socks.

Before the play begins, tell the audience where it is taking place and who the two characters represent.

Finally, get your salesman and your customer onstage and let them act things out! You will be pleased at the way in which they build an interesting play for you. Let the customer ask questions about the product. Let the salesman show the customer how the product works. Have the customer complain that the price is too high. Before long you will have dozens of good ideas which you can develop into a lively act.

FAMOUS PEOPLE

The idea is for a puppet or a group of puppets to impersonate famous people. The audience tries to guess who they are. The famous man or woman can be revealed by the puppet's words and actions. A single puppet could impersonate Benjamin Franklin by pretending to fly a kite while remarking about electricity. Two puppets could come onstage and act out a scene which revealed them as George and Martha Washington.

PUPPETS FROM HISTORY

You can build a very interesting act around great moments in history. Keep the performance fairly short and simple. It is best to choose scenes which do not require too many puppets. A few examples:

1. Thomas A. Edison works with one or two assistants to invent the electric light.

2. Christopher Columbus listens to the complaints of his sailors, but a few moments later they break into cheers as the New World is sighted.

WILD WEST SHOW

A show about the wild west is certain to be popular with your audience. It is especially suitable for a large group of puppeteers. A wide *Blanket Theater* (explained in the first pages of this book) is best for staging a western scene. Several types of puppets (also explained in the first pages) can be made and used.

Build your show around familiar actions of the wild west. The show could open as a pair of covered wagons bump onto the stage. Next, some cowboys or soldiers could enter on horseback as guards. Bison could rush onstage briefly and disappear. Then, some Indians could attack the covered wagons. Simple actions like these will make an exciting show that can last for several minutes.

You can include the following characters and animals and moving objects:

1. cowboys
2. soldiers
3. Indians
4. women
5. children
6. horses
7. sheep
8. bison
9. cattle
10. train
11. stagecoach
12. covered wagons

DANCE AND JOKE

This is an old and favorite type of stage act which is just as popular today as it ever was. You can use it to put on an attractive act with puppets.

Two puppets take part. They can be two boys or two girls or one of each. The act proceeds as the puppets alternate between dancing and joking. In other words, the performers dance for a bit, then stop long enough to exchange funny conversation, then dance once more. They alternate between dancing and joking for as long as the act continues.

The dance can consist of almost anything, just as long as it is light and peppy. All sorts of varieties can be used, such as dancing back to back and by having them alternate back and forth with one stretching upward and the other crouching. The dancing part should be accompanied by music. The music starts and stops as the puppets dance and stop.

Two or three jokes are enough for exchange during each pause in the dancing. Jokes and riddles can be found in books and magazines.

WHAT LANGUAGE?

This one makes a fun-filled series of short acts in which the audience can take part. The viewers are told that the acts will include just two or three sentences of dialogue. While puppets will speak in English, the audience must try to guess the language which is correctly associated with the performance.

As an example of how an act might be worked out, two puppets come onstage. One of them starts working. The other puppet asks him, "What are you doing?" The working puppet replies, "I'm repairing this wall." The audience might then guess that the correct language is Chinese, inasmuch as the Great Wall is in China. As another example, one puppet might ask another, "Where do you live?" The other puppet answers, "In the city of the Eiffel Tower." Since the Eiffel Tower is in Paris, the language would be French.

The following languages will make good scenes:

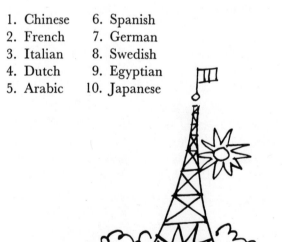

1. Chinese
2. French
3. Italian
4. Dutch
5. Arabic
6. Spanish
7. German
8. Swedish
9. Egyptian
10. Japanese

HELPFUL PUPPETS

Puppet-people are ready and willing to teach us the lessons we need to learn for healthy and happy living. Why not build a show or stunt around a useful idea? The stunt entitled *Crash* on another page of this book is a good example of how you can build one.

Here are twenty topics which can be developed into useful and attractive shows:

1. traffic safety
2. thriftiness
3. good study habits
4. forest preservation
5. fair play
6. correct eating habits
7. reading of books
8. self-reliance
9. dental care
10. friendliness
11. proper sleeping habits
12. patriotism
13. good manners
14. personal neatness
15. promptness
16. good working habits
17. cooperation
18. safety in the home
19. good posture
20. building of courage

5. Pantomime Plays
for Puppets

You will be surprised at what superb pantomime artists puppets can be. The ideas in this section will show you how to present attractive puppet plays in pantomime.

No words are spoken by the actors or actresses during a pantomime act. They perform in silence. They tell the story of the play by their actions and gestures. However, it is always effective to include background music in the play. Also, you can add sound effects to help develop the drama.

Your puppets should perform simple movements that the viewers understand clearly. Puppeteers should check their play from time to time during rehearsal to make sure that the pantomime movements are easy to understand.

This section offers you a wide variety of acts. Some of them make use of a narrator who speaks to the audience as the actors perform in silence. The purpose of a narrator is to help the audience understand the onstage action.

CHARADE PUPPETS

Here is a very special way to have fun with puppets. Your audience takes part in the play. The idea is for the puppet (or puppets) to lead the audience in a game of charades. Charades is a game in which a secret word is acted out for the audience to guess. No words are spoken by the actor; he reveals the secret word by acts and motions.

For your puppet charades use very simple words. Also, choose words that the puppet can reveal through simple actions. For example, if the puppeteer chose the secret word of *whirl*, he would enter the stage and whirl around. If the audience guessed the word *spin*, or maybe *turn*, the puppet would shake his head and whirl some more. Before too long the audience will guess that the secret word is *whirl*.

Two puppets can come onstage and act out the same word. The audience should be told beforehand that both actors are going to be doing the same thing.

Here is a list of good words to use:

1.	bounce	11.	shiver
2.	yes	12.	fall
3.	sleep	13.	hop
4.	dance	14.	sway
5.	slow	15.	fast
6.	run	16.	stumble
7.	bow	17.	leap
8.	jump	18.	fly
9.	no	19.	knock
10.	retreat	20.	exercise

TUG-OF-WAR

Here is a favorite picnic stunt that you can perform onstage with entertaining results. You can present the act using four puppets, or only two, so long as you have an equal number on both sides.

Before the puppets appear onstage fasten a length of cord to them in a way that makes it appear that the puppets are grasping the rope. This prevents the rope from slipping off during the tugging. Small safety pins will usually serve the purpose.

Use your imagination to think of clever actions for the puppet-athletes. Here are some good suggestions:

1. Let them tug back and forth as if one side is winning, then the other.

2. Let one side pull so hard that they move backward into the wing and off the stage completely, then have their opponents struggle back to do the same in the opposite wing.

3. Let one side collapse so that the puppets are dragged across the stage for awhile.

4. Let them tug in rhythm to offstage music.

5. Let one side pull its opponents offstage so swiftly that all of them shoot into the wing with a loud crash.

SHIPS AT SEA

Your ships are the stars of this show! You can build a very entertaining pantomime act by sending to sea some boats of different shapes and sizes. There is something fascinating about ships that sail and dip upon the ocean—especially when you include background music and sound effects.

Draw several kinds of boats on thick paper or thin cardboard. Cut them out and color them brightly. (Or, you can clip pictures from magazines no longer being used.) Paste each ship onto the end of a long and narrow stick. Hold the other end of the stick and let the ship appear above the stage as if sailing over the water.

Let your ships move around with various actions. Here are ten suggestions:

1. A pair of ships race each other.
2. A tugboat helps a passenger liner into port.
3. Ships struggle as if in a violent storm.
4. A man floats by on a raft.
5. A whale chases a ship around the stage.
6. A submarine comes up and goes down.
7. A speedy motorboat races around a slow sailboat.

8. A pirate ship and a modern ship pass each other.
9. Two ships turn and dip in unison.
10. Several ships speed onstage and off furiously.

STORY ACTS

In this type of pantomime a narrator tells a story to the audience at the same time that the puppets act it out. The narrator can remain hidden from the audience by standing behind the stage, or he can stand in view and to one side of the stage where he can see the action.

Fairy tales and ancient myths are especially good for story acts. Sound effects will help to make the acts interesting.

BUSY BOULEVARD

Cars zip past each other!

A traffic policeman blows his whistle at a speeding motorist!

Pedestrians dodge the traffic!

That is the kind of exciting action you can expect when your pantomime show takes place on a busy boulevard. Stick puppets are best for this pantomime act because you will want to use a great many puppets. Here are a few kinds of puppet-people you can place on the boulevard:

1. drivers in automobiles
2. drivers in trucks
3. men on motorcycles
4. pedestrians
5. policeman
6. policeman in police car
7. passengers on bus
8. firemen on fire truck

The best way for the puppeteers to build the act is to think of what actually happens in heavy traffic—and then exaggerate everything, including the speed of the vehicles. You can develop dozens of interesting movements, such as pedestrians dodging in and out, drivers shaking their fists at each other, and so on.

Sound effects are very important to the show. Assistants can stand in back of the puppeteers and add the sounds that you hear in heavy traffic.

THE MAGIC MIRROR

This clever idea will give you extra use of the puppets which you have made for other shows. It offers brief roles for ten or more puppets. This pantomime play employs a narrator who is a puppet himself.

The puppet who narrates the act is an inventor who is dressed in a smock. He enters and introduces himself as Gregory Q. Genius, the world-famous inventor. He announces that he has just invented a magic mirror. This magic mirror, he says, can instantly change a person into someone else. The only thing a person has to do is to walk in front of it and *bang*! The person is changed instantly into someone or something else.

The inventor then faces a screen which has been set up at the center of the stage. He says that the magic mirror is behind the screen. He tells the audience that his magic mirror has been set up on a busy sidewalk where lots of people pass by. "Let's see what happens," he says finally, "as people are changed by my magic mirror."

The inventor stands aside. A puppet enters from the right wing and passes in back of the screen. As soon as he disappears behind it he is quickly replaced by another puppet who comes out on the other side of the screen. He exits at the left wing.

One after another, several puppet-persons walk in back of the screen where they are replaced by other puppet-people. You can make all sorts of amusing switches. For instance, a man can turn into a prancing goat, or a horse can come out as a bouncing clown.

To finish the act, the inventor announces that he himself will also walk before the mirror. He then goes behind the screen and comes out as some funny sort of creature, perhaps a monkey. He shrugs and remarks to the audience, "All I can say is, be sure to watch out for the magic mirror!" He scampers offstage as the curtain falls.

FISHING

The way in which a puppet theater is built is the reason why this amusing stunt is possible. Two or three puppets can take part. They are assisted by stagehands who also remain out of sight behind the theater.

The pantomime opens as the puppet-fishermen sit or stand facing the audience. Their fishing lines are fastened to their arms so that they can swing them up and down. The lines are just long enough to reach out of sight below the stage floor. A piece of bent wire, serving as a hook, is attached to the end of each line.

The following kinds of actions make this a lively play:

1. The fishermen constantly catch all sorts of odd and funny items, such as a cookie, a peanut, a flower, a spool, and miniature toys.

These objects are attached to the hooks by the assistants when the puppets lean forward to lower the lines. As a puppet leans back, the line is raised to reveal the object to the audience. When the line is once more lowered the first object is removed and another hooked on.

The puppets can react to their strange catches by fainting, shaking, and turning to look at each other with shock.

2. For a second series of actions, have an assistant tug on a fishing line as if a large fish had caught his hook. They struggle

back and forth. The puppet finally flies outward toward the audience for a few inches, then plunges downward and out of sight as if yanked by the fish. The puppet reappears and fishes once more.

You can use this idea in several ways. Have all the fishermen disappear at once. Have them disappear one after another in quick succession. Have one of them dip up and down rapidly several times.

For a humorous finish, have a large fish-puppet poke its open mouth upward toward the fishermen. They jerk back and race offstage.

THE CHASERS

For exciting action, there is nothing like puppets who chase each other around the stage! With a little imagination you can build a peppy play out of chasing performers.

The first step is to decide upon the kind of puppets who will chase each other. Here are five examples:

1. man and bear
2. dog and cat
3. cowboy and Indian
4. eagle and wolf
5. kangaroo and soldier

Next, think of different things that could happen as they run around. They might suddenly drop below the stage as if falling into a river. They can alternate in chasing each other. The puppet being chased might stop so suddenly that the pursuing puppet crashes into him. Once you get your puppets onstage you will be able to come up with lots of ideas for action.

Music is especially good for this type of show. Play a lively phonograph record as the puppets perform.

You can start the show with an introduction something like this: "Ladies and gentlemen, you will now see some exciting action as a cowboy chases an Indian—and as the Indian does some chasing, too!"

THE KEEP-TRYING MAN

This pantomime is narrated by a player who may stand in view of the audience or who may remain hidden. The important idea is for the narrator to speak clearly and in harmony with the onstage action.

The words and actions given below are written for a puppet performance. However, it is also suitable for real actors and actresses. In the puppet performance, the puppets appear and disappear from below the stage. In a show for real players, the performers crouch onstage as if hiding, then stretch up and down as directed in the instructions given below.

The narrator's words can be memorized or simply read from this book. As soon as he speaks a sentence, the players carry out the actions as instructed:

"Once upon a time there was a man with a camera . . ." (The puppet comes onstage, carrying a camera. He bows to audience, remains facing it.)

"He was a man who liked to keep trying to take pictures . . ." (He moves himself and his camera from left to right and back.)

"He was a man who liked especially to keep trying to take pictures of wild animals . . . "(As the puppet looks straight ahead toward the audience, the animals pop up in unison from below the stage just long enough for a bow, then disappear downward. There should be either two or four animals altogether, one or two on each side of the puppet-man.)

"One day the man who liked to keep trying to take pictures of wild animals went for a hike in the woods . . ." (The man walks in a circle.)

"As the man who liked to keep trying to take pictures of wild animals walked in the woods he looked around for wild animals to take pictures of . . ." (The man walks in a circle, looking around.)

"He looked toward the east, but saw no wild animals . . ."

(As the man looks toward the right, the animals pop up at the left, then disappear downward.)

"He looked toward the west, but saw nothing . . ." (As he looks toward the left, the animals pop up at right, then disappear.)

"He looked up into the trees, but saw no wild animals . . ." (As he looks upward, the animals pop up near his legs, then disappear.)

"He looked down into the caves, but saw nothing at all . . ." (As he looks downward, the animals appear overhead by hanging down from the top of the stage, then disappear upward. Note: If the play is performed by real actors in pantomime, eliminate this action.)

"Wherever he looked, the man who liked to keep trying to take pictures of wild animals could see no wild animals that he could take pictures of . . ." (The man looks rapidly in succession toward the four previous directions.)

"This made him so very sad that he cried like this . . ." (He bends forward and shakes as if sobbing.)

"But because he was a man who liked to keep trying to take pictures of wild animals, he decided to keep trying to take pictures of wild animals . . ." (While keeping his back to the audience, the man searches around upstage.)

"And that is when something interesting happened . . ." (The animals pop up and huddle together downstage to talk.)

"The wild animals decided that because the man who liked to keep trying to take pictures of wild animals was the kind of a man who kept trying to take pictures of wild animals that they would help him to take pictures of wild animals . . ." (All the animals disappear downward.)

"So the next time the man looked toward the east he saw a wild animal . . ." (As he looks toward the right, an animal pops up.)

"When he looked toward the west he saw another wild animal . . ." (As he looks toward the left, an animal appears.)

"He looked upward and there was another one . . ." (As he looks upward, an animal appears by hanging overhead.)

"And when he looked downward he saw another wild animal . . ." (As he looks downward, an animal appears close to his face.)

"No matter where he looked, the man who liked to keep trying to take pictures of wild animals always saw wild animals . . ." (The animals appear anywhere onstage.)

"This made him so very happy that he laughed like this . . ." (He shakes back and forth as if laughing merrily.)

"This also made the wild animals so very happy that they also laughed like this . . ." (The animals also shake back and forth in merry laughter.)

"Everyone agreed that it is always a good idea to keep trying to do whatever you want to do . . ." (Everyone onstage nods toward the audience. The curtain falls.)

MARCHING SOLDIERS

It is a fascinating sight to watch puppet-soldiers march around the stage! The audience is certain to like the way they step around in rhythm to peppy music. Try the following ideas for building a show of marching puppets:

1. Stick puppets make wonderful soldiers and are easy to create. Draw pictures of soldiers on stiff paper. Then cut the figures out and paste them on stick handles.

2. Have the soldiers march in time with the music by bouncing up and down as they march.

3. For humorous action, have your soldiers march down the left wall of the stage, march across the stage, then march up the right wall. When they reach the top of the wall, pull the puppets offstage and let them appear once more from the floor of the stage.

4. Have all the soldiers break formation and march individually in any direction. They march back and forth across the stage while passing each other.

5. Let all the soldiers line up facing the audience. Have them sway sideways, back and forth, in rhythm to the music.

6. Let the soldiers march around in single file.

7. Have them line up facing the audience, while bouncing up and down only slightly. The first soldier in line starts to bounce up and down vigorously. In turn, the other puppets do the same. As soon as all of them are bouncing with vigor, they march away into another stunt.

8. Let the soldiers march offstage and march back again. This can be performed two or three times.

9. Leave just two of the soldiers onstage to perform for awhile. For one of their stunts, have them march straight toward each other and dodge a collision at the very last moment.

10. The soldiers march offstage as the music concludes.

THE WALL

Prepare for this act by setting up a paper wall on the stage. Let it run from upstage to downstage, a short distance from the left wing. It should be somewhat higher than the puppets as they appear onstage.

A narrator explains the action to the audience as a pair of puppets act it out:

"Once upon a time there were two enthusiastic travelers . . ." (The puppets bounce merrily onstage from the right wing.)

"One morning the two enthusiastic travelers were traveling toward a big city when they suddenly came to a big wall . . ." (The puppets walk to the wall and stop.)

"The big wall was a big problem to the two travelers because they did not know how to get to the other side of such a big wall . . ." (The puppets look up to the top of the wall and shake their heads.)

"One of the travelers decided to try to get to the other side of the wall by digging beneath it . . ." (Puppet A bends back and forth at the base of the wall as if digging.)

"But the wall was much too thick for him . . ." (The puppet sags and falls to the ground.)

"The other traveler decided to try to jump over the wall . . ." (Puppet B runs and jumps in swift action in an effort to get over the wall.)

"But the wall was much too high for him . . ." (The puppet collapses and falls down.)

"But the enthusiastic travelers made up their minds that the thick and high wall was not going to defeat them . . ." (The puppets leap up and nod their heads vigorously.)

"They knew there had to be a way to get over the wall and they also knew that they could find it . . ." (The puppets nod with even more vigor.)

"They agreed to travel to a library and read a book entitled *How You Can Get on the Other Side of a Thick and High Wall* . . ." (The puppets exit at right.)

"They were very wise in reading that book because it told them exactly how to get on the other side of a thick and high wall . . ." (The puppets enter from right while nodding.)

"The enthusiastic travelers knew that they would only hurt themselves by trying to dig under the wall . . ." (Puppet A digs briefly, faces the audience and shakes his head.)

"And they knew that there was a much better way than to try to jump over the wall . . ." (Puppet B briefly tries to jump the wall, then faces the audience and shakes his head.)

"They discovered that there is a right way to do everything . . ." (The puppets nod in unison.)

"They discovered especially that there is a right way to get on the other side of a thick and high wall . . ." (The puppets nod with vigor.)

"So here is how they did things in the right way and got to the other side of that thick and high wall . . ." (The puppets crouch briefly, then crash through the paper wall and bounce offstage at left.)

CRASH

Here is a short act which is especially good for teaching safety. The announcer tells the audience that they will be shown why they should not run while indoors. The announcer then stands aside as a puppet races in from the left wing, dashes across the stage and exits at right. Another puppet enters from the right and races across to exit at left. The first puppet enters from the right and races offstage at the left. The second puppet runs on from the left and exits at the right. Then, both puppets race onstage from opposite wings and crash together in the center, accompanied by the sound effects of a loud crash. They fall, slowly get up, and stagger dizzily offstage in opposite directions.

PANTOMIME CIRCUS

Put on a puppet circus in pantomime! Back up the onstage action with a phonograph record that plays a lively military march. You are sure to have a hit.

Prepare as many puppets as you like in the costumes of circus performers. Here are a few you can use:

1. clown
2. acrobat
3. cowboy
4. Indian
5. lady dancer
6. popcorn salesman
7. horse
8. elephant
9. seal
10. lion and lion tamer

The puppet-performers come onstage in any order and perform according to their characters. The clown bounces merrily around, the lion trainer snaps a whip at the lion, and the dancer glides gracefully about. They perform briefly, then exit, and then return for another brief performance. The action should be continuous. Two or three puppets can be onstage at the same time.

BEST FRIENDS

You can use puppets from other shows for this amusing act, both human figures and animals. The greater the variety you have, the better the act will be.

A puppet comes onstage as the announcer. He informs the audience that the puppets of this theater have formed some close friendships. He goes on to say that everyone in the group has found a best friend—and that some of the couples are very interesting to see. The announcer remarks that it might be fun to watch the couples as they meet each other. The announcer calls out, "Here they come!" and races offstage.

Here is an example of the action that now takes place: A puppet comes onstage from the right wing, looks into the left wing as if seeing someone, then waves happily. From offstage the announcer calls out, "Best friend!" Another puppet races in from the left wing and another voice offstage calls out, "Best friend!" They embrace each other and walk offstage together.

The above action is repeated several times with different pairs of puppets. In other words, a puppet enters, calls out, and waits expectantly. The other puppet then rushes onstage and returns the greeting. After embracing, the puppets walk offstage together.

The idea that makes the act amusing is the odd combinations of best friends, so be sure to make them as different as possible. Here are five examples:

1. A boy and a whale
2. A princess and a mule
3. A tall man and short man.
4. A fish and a bird.
5. A girl and a dragon.

The puppets can come onstage from the wings or from above or below the stage. Animals can appear from below the stage as if coming from underground, while birds can swoop down from the top of the stage.

THE QUICK-CHANGE ARTIST

You would have to search long and far to find an act as delightfully clever as this one. It makes full use of some of the advantages of using puppets as actresses and actors.

The show is based on the fact that a puppeteer can switch swiftly from one puppet to another. The change of puppets is seen by the audience as a change of costume by a single puppet who is a quick-change artist. In other words, although a number of puppets appear in the act, they are supposed to be the same puppet in different costumes and characters.

The program starts as the announcer (or the puppet himself in a one-man show) informs the audience that they are about to see a quick-change artist in action. The puppet enters and bows to the audience. He performs a little dance or stunt and meanwhile the announcer says that the performer will show how quickly he can change from one costume to another.

The puppet races offstage. Then he enters seconds later wearing a completely different costume and bows to the viewers. He then exits and, in his original costume, the puppet returns to the stage for another bow. He remains onstage for the next announcement.

Of course, the puppeteer doesn't have to change the puppet's clothes. He simply switches to another puppet with the same face and shape but wearing another kind of costume altogether.

For the second act the puppet can perform a whole series of speedy switches in costume. The puppet dashes offstage and back several times, each time in a different outfit. Two puppeteers can work together to make the changes rapid and smooth. In that way you won't need so many puppets. While one of the puppets is onstage, another actually gets a new costume. Finally, the original puppet returns and bows several times.

For act three, the puppet bows, runs offstage and returns a moment later as the very same puppet with no changes made

whatsoever! The announcer explains with a smile that the puppet is so speedy that while offstage he changed into six other costumes and still had time to change back to his own. The puppet bows happily in several directions.

The grand finale is the most fantastic of all. Two or three puppeteers work at racing several different puppets onstage and off. They can enter from either wing, or hang down from the ceiling or pop up from below the stage. Two or three should appear at the same time. Some of them need not look like the original puppet at all. In fact, you can even include animals and birds. Finally, the original puppet appears alone onstage for final bows and the announcer leads the audience in applause.

6. Pantomimes for Real Actors and Actresses

Inasmuch as no words are ever spoken during a pantomime play you do not have to memorize dialogue for the acts in this section. However, it is an interesting challenge to an actor or actress to see how cleverly he or she can put over a silent scene. You can accomplish more than you may think by the correct use of facial expressions and by gestures and movements.

One of the most helpful ways to learn the art of pantomime is to handle real objects and then practice the same movements with imaginary items. As an example, perform the simple act of taking a book from a table, glancing through a few pages, then returning it to the table. As you do this with the real book, keep noticing the movements of your hands and eyes and head. Next, practice the same actions without a book and see how closely you can duplicate the movements. This is the kind of practice that turns you into a skillful pantomime artist.

Most pantomime acts are performed without the use of stage properties, though you can use a few when necessary. Simple objects such as a chair, or a box representing a television set may be used, but you wouldn't use a real needle when pantomiming someone sewing.

Your audience takes part in many of the silent scenes found in this section, for often the viewers try to guess the kind of action that the actors and actresses are pantomiming.

PRODUCTS IN PANTOMIME

This idea will make it fun for actors and actresses to develop their skill in the art of pantomime. Each player selects one of the well-known products listed below. Then he acts out a scene in pantomime in which he uses the product in some way. An actor who chose glass could pretend to polish an imaginary window pane; another actor could use a sponge by pantomiming the act of dipping a sponge into a pail of water and then squeezing it out.

1.	glass	11.	copper
2.	sponge	12.	wool
3.	tin	13.	feathers
4.	leather	14.	gold
5.	silk	15.	aluminum
6.	oil	16.	cotton
7.	lumber	17.	ivory
8.	iron	18.	lead
9.	cork	19.	fur
10.	rubber	20.	silver

The audience attempts to guess the product. As soon as it is correctly identified, another performer goes onstage.

THE TALKERS

A pair of performers face each other onstage. They talk to each other in pantomime, with plenty of gestures, body actions and facial expressions. A speaker's mouth may move as if talking, but he must not make sounds.

The talkers try to reveal to the audience their subject of conversation. The audience watches their pantomime movements in an effort to guess what it is. The viewers continue to make guesses throughout the performance until the actors inform them of a correct guess.

The selected topic should be one that offers lots of opportunities for pantomime action. Here are fifteen that will serve the purpose:

1. clothing
2. airplanes
3. the weather
4. music
5. sleep
6. gardening
7. dancing
8. money
9. the sea
10. candy
11. school
12. jewelry
13. the time
14. flowers
15. an athletic contest

IN THE DARK

This act offers a double reward: It is good for practicing the art of pantomime acting. It is fun to watch!

The idea is for a performer to pretend that he is groping in the dark. Actually he can see where he is going but he pretends to stumble, to bump into things and so forth. Each player thinks up two separate things to do—or that happen to him—while groping in the dark. They need not necessarily be funny events, but they should be as interesting as possible.

The audience is told whether the act is taking place indoors or outdoors. Here are good examples of both:

1. He bumps into a door and bangs his nose.
2. He falls into a swimming pool.
3. He finds his coat and puts it on.
4. He plunges his hand into a sticky pie.
5. He stubs his toe on a cat which he picks up and pets.
6. He tries to thread a needle but misses by a foot.
7. He tries to eat but misses his mouth constantly.
8. He bumps into a freshly painted wall.
9. He tries to iron clothes.
10. He turns on the water sprinkler and gets wet.

The actor performs his actions as clearly as possible. When he finishes, the audience tries to guess what they were. Sometimes this is the most laughable part of the act.

SCREAMS

This is a surprise act for the performers as well as the audience. It is certain to cause everyone to explode with laughter. Clever sound effects will help put it over with a bang.

The announcer tells the performers that they are about to discover a savage lion in the living room. Of course, anyone who comes upon the savage king of beasts is bound to scream. But, the announcer continues, the scream must be done in pantomime. No actual sounds should be uttered. The player must open his mouth and throw up his arms as if to scream, but—the actual sounds will be supplied by a crew handling the sound effects!

One by one each player comes onstage, walks a few steps, opens an imaginary door and pretends to see the savage lion. Then he must pantomime the act of screaming wildly.

The funny part happens when he pretends to scream. The sound crew adds the sound effect, but instead of a scream they use all sorts of peculiar sounds. Here are examples: blow a whistle, crash pans together several times, pop a paper sack filled with air, rip a newspaper, ring a bell, play briefly and sharply on a musical instrument. The sound crew can also use their own voices by shrieking and howling, or even giggling.

Correct timing is important. At the instant that the player pantomimes his scream, the sound should be added.

THE EXPERTS

This outdoor scene opens with two seated performers opposite each other, playing a game of checkers. Their backs are to the wings.

As they silently study the checker board, a passer-by enters while reading a newspaper. As he approaches the players he glances over and sees the game, so he stops to watch. Just as player A is about to make a move, the passer-by shakes his head in solemn disapproval and grabs player A's hand, preventing the move. The passer-by then motions for player A to stand aside for a moment. As player A does so, the passer-by sits down, studies the board for a moment, then makes a non-jumping move. Nodding in satisfaction, the passer-by stands and permits player A to return to the chair.

The passer-by remains to watch the game. Player B then makes his move, a non-jumping one.

The above actions are repeated two or three more times as other passers-by stop and make the moves for player A. After each passer-by has finished his move he stays to watch the game. Player B makes a non-jumping move after each passer-by has moved.

Finally, the last passer-by makes his move and stands up to

watch. Players A and B silently study the board for a moment, then player B slowly and solemnly makes six long jumps all over the board.

Player A stares at the board in silent shock for a moment, then looks up with a fierce expression at the passers-by. The passers-by look dismayed. Player A suddenly leaps up, scatters the board and checkers, and chases the passers-by offstage.

SPELL IT

A pair of performers select a secret word. Start out by using 4-letter words. They take turns in acting out other words which start with the letters in the secret word. If the secret word happened to be *cake*, the first player could act out a word that begins with the letter *c*, for example, *chair*. The other player would then act out the second letter, *a;* he might, for instance, act out the word *arrow*.

As each letter is guessed, someone writes it down on a blackboard or on a large sheet of paper. Before long the audience will be ready to guess longer words.

LOST AND FOUND

As many players as desired can take part in this comical pantomime stunt, although only two of them are onstage at a time.

The audience is told that the action takes place in the lost-and-found department of a police station. At the start of the performance a policeman (or policewoman) is on duty at a desk. One by one the players come onstage to tell the officer what has been lost. The performer describes the lost object by pantomime. For example, he can indicate a toy balloon by pretending to blow up a balloon. Then he can tap it with a finger to bounce it in the air.

The audience continues to guess until it names the lost object correctly. You can use the following items or make up your own.

1. a toy balloon
2. a canoe
3. a railroad ticket
4. a dog collar
5. a blanket
6. a flashlight
7. an anchor
8. a flute
9. a can of sardines
10. a door hinge
11. a baby's bottle
12. a bowl of goldfish
13. a mask
14. a puppet
15. a flag
16. a television aerial
17. a pet goat
18. a penny
19. a towel
20. a thermometer
21. a mirror
22. a postage stamp
23. a clock
24. an automobile tire
25. a cash register
26. a beehive
27. a mop
28. a king's crown
29. a statue
30. a block of ice

MIXED EMOTIONS

The audience takes part in this amusing stunt. Two performers come onstage. One of them silently acts out one of the paired words listed below, while the other performer acts out the other word. The audience is told that the emotions that they are to guess are opposites, such as gay and sad. Some of them will be easy for the audience to guess, while others will make them think twice. If the viewers do not guess both emotions within a reasonable time, the actors exchange words with each other and act them out again.

1. gay and sad
2. calm and excited
3. interested and indifferent
4. frightened and confident
5. hot and cold
6. energetic and tired
7. friendly and angry
8. peaceful and worried
9. certain and puzzled
10. relaxed and tense
11. nonchalant and surprised
12. fascinated and bored

NEWSPAPER DRAMATICS

This idea is good for a large number of performers. A small group of players or one single performer can pantomime each act.

Clip several news stories from the paper and give one to each group of players, or each individual. After reading the story they must act it out in pantomime and the others must try to guess what the story is about.

The pantomime act should not try to cover all the details of the story; only the central idea need be acted out. For instance, if the story concerns a railroad engine that spilled off its track, the story should be simplified to cover just that single point.

The players may repeat their pantomime once or twice. If the audience cannot guess within a reasonable time, tell them and go on to the next act.

THE MECHANICAL MAN

A mechanical man who is missing a few parts of his machinery can be one of the funniest sights ever seen on your stage!

The cast consists of two performers. One of them acts the pantomime role of the mechanical man, while the other player is his employer who gives the orders. The scene is a home. The action takes place as the employer tries to get the not-so-bright mechanical man to perform simple tasks around the house, such as dusting the furniture and cleaning the windows.

The pantomime begins as the employer pretends to call his servant. The robot enters the room by walking stiffly and with short and jerky steps. His arms swing with tight and precise movements; his face has a frozen expression.

The employer then tries to put his employee to work by pantomiming what he wants done. He pretends to sweep the floor, but the machine-man kneels down and sweeps with his hands. The performers can repeat this once or twice.

The employer pantomimes washing dishes and the mechanical man nods stiffly. He turns and stamps slowly offstage. A moment later a loud crash is heard. As the employer stares in shock, the mechanical man enters with bits of broken dishes (from cardboard plates) in his hands.

Let your machine-man continue in a series of funny actions like these for five or six minutes. He is worth lots of laughs.

BACKWARD PEOPLE

Be sure that you explain this one to the audience before the play begins!

Things go backward!

The whole idea is to build a pantomime act in which the actors and actresses perform a number of things in reverse of the usual way. For instance, instead of shaking hands when meeting, the players wave good-by.

As many players as desired can take part in the pantomime. Some can remain onstage during the whole performance, while others can enter and exit. The scene can take place in any location that offers opportunities for people to move around, such as a home, a schoolroom or a business office.

The best way to build a number of amusing backward actions is to think of a usual movement, then see if it is one that can be reversed. Try these ideas:

1. A player enters without a raincoat or an overcoat, finds one and wears it while working at a desk.

2. The players walk backward.

3. A performer opens a box containing a hat, throws the hat aside and wears the box on his head.

4. A couple dance briefly, back to back and holding hands.

5. A boy dives into the water. Then he takes off shoes and socks.

6. A girl comes into the room, opens her umbrella and holds it over her head. Then she closes it and goes out.

7. A player pours water from a drinking glass into a pitcher and drinks from the pitcher.

8. A player clears an imaginary dinner table, then sits down and eats.

TENNIS MATCH

The pantomime version of a tennis match can make a highly entertaining act. Two or four players can take part.

The performers stand facing each other with their backs to the wings. An imaginary net runs down the center of the stage from upstage to downstage. The tennis balls and rackets are imaginary.

The main idea to remember as the ball goes back and forth is to exaggerate everything. When a player leaps to hit the ball he should leap wildly; when he swings at the ball he should swing with smashing swiftness. The facial expressions should also be exaggerated. This means that when a player is pleased with himself he pantomimes a broad laugh; when he is disappointed with his game his whole face and body sag.

Many amusing actions can be included, such as falling down, striking the ball with the knee, and swinging the racket with both hands as if it were a baseball bat.

The players can make the ball seem very real by keeping their eyes on its imaginary flight back and forth. They should also watch the timing of the ball and not strike too soon.

That is, they should allow for the time a ball would normally take in traveling back and forth. During this time, they can be reacting to it and racing after it.

When there are two players on each side, the teammates should alternate in returning the ball.

MEN OF MARS

Here is a nonsense pantomime that calls for a wild imagination—the wilder the better! An announcer tells the audience that a spaceship has just returned from the planet Mars, full of people who have been studying the Martians. The announcer says that the Martian people have some odd ways of walking down the street, which the actors and actresses will demonstrate.

One by one the performers move across the stage in all sorts of peculiar ways. Here are five suggestions:

1. Cross by shuffling both feet which are set inside cardboard grocery cartons.

2. Cross by pausing every fourth step to blow a whistle while hopping up and down in place.

3. Cross while holding a pillow against the head as if sleeping.

4. Cross while sweeping the floor with the wrong end of a broom.

5. Cross while staring intently at a single large flower which is held by both hands in front of the face.

SLOW-MOTION PANTOMIME

There is something especially entertaining about a pantomime that is performed in slow-motion. It may be difficult sometimes for the players to keep from laughing during the act, but that is all part of the fun. Two or more performers can take roles.

Select an act that offers plenty of opportunity for physical movements. It should consist of a scene that is familiar to the audience, such as playing tennis or checking out groceries at the market or perhaps a classroom activity.

Once the act has been more or less worked out, the performers should rehearse it at normal speed to get acquainted with the basic movements. The players then repeat the pantomime more and more slowly, until they have it in slow-motion.

There are two special ways to make a slow-motion pantomime as amusing as possible. First, choose funny physical movements such as these two examples: *a.* A golfer spins slowly around several times after giving the ball a terrific whack; he spins again and sinks to the ground in exhaustion. *b.* A waiter tries desperately to balance several imaginary dishes in his hand; as they spill, he desperately grabs the air, trying to catch them before they smash on the floor.

The other important thing is to build the expression on your face slowly. Whenever something happens, build up your facial expression a little at a time until it is quite exaggerated. For instance, the waiter would grow more and more terrified as he grabs at his imaginary dishes.

Keep your slow-motion pantomime short and punchy.

DIRECTIONS

This pantomime act can bring all sorts of chuckles and giggles from the audience. All it takes is a clever performance!

Each player finds a partner. They work the act out together. One of them plays the role of a lost pedestrian who asks for directions from the other, a local resident. This situation offers endless opportunities for pantomime comedy at its best.

The act begins as the lost pedestrian approaches the local resident and asks him (in pantomime, of course) for directions for reaching a certain place. He can ask his questions by making gestures or by pointing to an address on an imaginary letter. Also, he can show how helpless he is by shrugging his shoulders and by frowning.

The local resident then replies by pantomiming some fantastic instructions. He can indicate left and right turns; he can get down and crawl to indicate that this is what the other man must do; he can make swimming motions as if there is a lake which must be crossed. The whole idea is to make the directions as strange and as comical as possible.

Of course, the lost pedestrian goes into some reactions to the directions. He can droop in dismay. He can scratch his head. He can start off as if following the directions and then come back in utter confusion for more instructions.

The act concludes as the lost pedestrian finally staggers offstage into one of the wings, while the local resident strolls happily off into the opposite wing.

In turn, each couple presents their version of the act.

SILLY SIGHTS

Everyone thinks up a silly sight which he might have seen, such as those listed below. One after another the performers act them out, while the others try to guess what they are. The audience keeps guessing as the act is performed, while the actor nods either *yes* or *no* to the guesses.

1. A laughing rabbit
2. A motorcycle with six wheels
3. A cat that walks backward
4. A green sun
5. A swimming camel
6. A red dollar bill
7. A crying ostrich
8. A talking scarecrow
9. A book that can be eaten
10. A man as tall as a tree
11. A flying dog
12. A square football
13. A dancing spoon
14. A cloud in a closet
15. A walking pencil
16. A whale in a goldfish bowl
17. A rowboat on the desert
18. A horse only five inches tall
19. A purple pig
20. A railroad track made of sugar

OPEN IT

In this guessing game the players pantomime the act of opening something, such as the objects listed below. The idea is to reveal to the audience the imaginary object which you are opening. For instance, a player could pick up a package of flower seeds, tear off a corner, sprinkle the seeds onto the ground and water them. Also, a performer could open a safety pin and use it to fasten parts of his clothing.

The players take a few minutes to practice their pantomimes. They then come onstage, one at a time, and let the audience guess the object which they are opening. If necessary, a player can repeat his act once or twice.

1. package of flower seeds
2. safety pin
3. wallet
4. candy bar
5. can of paint
6. Chinese fortune cookie
7. watermelon
8. photograph album
9. bottle of catsup
10. walnut
11. letter
12. jar of glue
13. umbrella
14. box of crackers
15. package of cough drops
16. woman's purse
17. can of shoe polish
18. safe
19. jar of vitamins
20. package of butter
21. cupboard
22. box of stationery
23. jar of peanut butter
24. tool box
25. first aid kit
26. filing cabinet
27. package of cheese
28. sewing kit
29. doctor's bag
30. box of laundry soap

INDEX